AF330084

POPPIES

POEMS BY
FLOYD SKLOOT

STORY LINE PRESS
SILVERFISH REVIEW PRESS

Grateful acknowledgement is made to the editors of the following magazines in which these poems first appeared:

The American Scholar: "Mendelssohn at Thirty-Eight"
Crazyhorse: "Coffee"
The Harvard Review: "Cape Lookout"
The Iowa Review: "Fires"
The New Criterion: "Currents"
New England Review: "Object Assembly"
Northwest Review: "Sage"
Poetry Northwest: "Ravel at Swim"
Prairie Schooner: "Dizzy" and "Touches"
Virginia Quarterly Review: "Delius & Fenby"
Willamette Week: "Dancing in the Cosmos"

"Dancing in the Cosmos" and "Poppies" originally appeared in *The Gettysburg Review,* volume 7, number 1, and "Paganini and the Powers of Darkness" appeared in volume 3, number 3. These poems are reprinted here by permission of the editors.

The poems "Ravel at Swim" and "Spring Storm" appeared in *JAMA: The Journal of the American Medical Association.*

"Dancing in the Cosmos" was reprinted in *Willamette Week.*

I would like to thank the Oregon Institute of Literary Arts for a Fellowship, and Centrum for a writing residency during which some of these poems were written.

ISBN: 0-934257-82-5 (Story Line Press)
ISBN: 1-878851-05-5 (Silverfish Review Press)

CONTENTS

Object Assembly 7
Spring Storm 9
Delius & Fenby 10
Ravel at Swim 13
Mendelssohn at Thirty-Eight 15
Paganini and the Powers of Darkness 16
Sage 17
Coffee 18
Fires 19
Touches 21
Dizzy 23
Lime at the Edges 24
Currents 26
Beautiful Lily 27
Poppies 28
Cape Lookout 29
Dancing in the Cosmos 30

FOR BEVERLY

"We are vulnerable because of our very intricacy and complexity. We are
systems of mechanisms, subject to all the small disturbances, tiny monkey
wrenches, that can, in the end, produce the wracking and unhinging
of interminable chains of coordinated, meticulously timed interaction."
—from "On Disease," by Lewis Thomas

OBJECT ASSEMBLY

"The most pronounced deficits were overall IQ;
visual sequencing; nonverbal problem-solving ability;
visual, spatial and fine motor functioning."
              —Dr. Sheila Bastien, "Neuropsychological
                    Deficits in Chronic Fatigue Syndrome"

They were five fingers and naked
fist palm down. They were wooden
bones too long in the grave, middle
and index still joined, the rest
adrift. They were a puzzle simple
as stark truth. He scattered them
before me, an offering from my own
future I could not assemble in time.

Nor could I assemble the Africa
that was a face without sense
organs, perhaps ears and nose
islands to the southeast, eye
afloat near Cape Verde. Time
was up before I found Madagascar.

Then I remembered summer dusks
spent shifting shades of blue
and red, hours finding patterns
centered around faded lilac
that became fields of fleur-de-lis
as jigsaw shape fitted to shape
and the familiar picture grew whole.
Monet came together in half
the time the box allowed.
My son, now the age I was then,
slapped hands across the card
table. Those days time was never
tight and my brain was intact.

Half a life later time reminds me
the temporal lobe scarred by virus
no longer functions as it should.
Rooms have walls in surprising
places and I get lost where I know
the way. These are called deficits.
Tests that would be games some other
time focus on what I cannot do.

So a Doctor of Psychology packs
the disassembled objects away beside
his blindfold and blocks I failed
to place in slots on a formboard
fast enough. He turns back to me,
knees to knees, flipping pictures
that have something missing I am
to name. I think the door should
have a wall around it but learn
later it should have had a knob.

Perhaps it is his face void
of expression, or his cracked
black bag of toys, or my young son
floating again near me with one
cerulean corner of sky cupped
in his palm. Perhaps I am tired.
But these tests at last reduce me
to tears like a child schneidered
by his father at gin rummy.

SPRING STORM

"What doesn't the wind lay claim to?"
—Rainer Maria Rilke

Scarlet tulip petals strewn by last night's
winds litter the gutter. Their colors still
vivid in a driving rain, they begin
to gather themselves like flaps of torn skin
closing where the culvert rises. Uphill
a pen holds freshly shorn sheep huddling white
in the middle of a flock—drenched and gray
as the sky—that runs past them on the way
to their morning feed as though astonished
at surviving what turned their mates to ghosts.
The brilliant yellow field of rape where Rice
Lane bends west in this light seems swollen twice
its former size and the stripped dogwood hosts
a family of mountain quail banished
by the storm. I have been sick for five years.
Walking through such mornings eases my fears.

DELIUS & FENBY

"To be a genius, as this man plainly was, and have
something beautiful in you and not be able to rid
yourself of it because you could no longer see
your score paper and no longer hold your pen—
well, the thought was unbearable!"
                          —Eric Fenby, *Delius As I Knew Him*

Always toward sunset Delius grew
restless and uneasy in his carriage
chair, raving at the pain in his legs,
flicking his long tapering fingers
as though stating a theme on the air.
His proud head, pale as marble,
began to wobble no matter the effort
to hold it still. He demanded a thick
rug for warmth. He demanded a thin rug
for comfort, then demanded that no
rug touch him, all the time wanting
me to read one more story aloud
like a child refusing to go to bed.

Delius required that everything
be just so. His bean and barley
soup must be salted in the pot
and served piping hot. No rattling
cups or clattering spoons at table,
where chitchat lashed him to fury.
After dinner, one cigar and a slow
push up the Marlotte road in silence,
when even the neighbor's great Alsatians
walked hushed beside us. Saturdays
we could play only Sir Thomas Beecham's
records of Delius on the gramophone
in the quiet of his music room.

One morning in the faded garden
where Delius sat beneath the elder
tree, I could see that he was angry
with me. Tossing his head from side
to side, he champed and glared
towad the rising sun, clearing
his throat *fortissimo.* At night
a melody had come on the verge
of sleep, making him weep to be
hearing new music leap in his mind
again. But I overslept beneath
the full-sized face of mad Strindberg
by Munch, dreaming myself south
to Paris amidst a wild summer storm,
surrounded by young friends in good
health, rain playing a sudden cadenza
on the swollen Somme and the thunder
in E-Flat. I wanted tea.

My hair still damp, my face creased
by sleep, I took up paper and pen
without a word. I sat cross-legged
on the grass wondering whether Delius
would sing to me. Would he call out
the notes and their time-values?
At last I was to do what I had come
from Scarborough to do and free him
of the music. He threw his head
back like a wild horse in flight
and neighed toneless to the sky.
"Hold it!" he said, causing me
to drop my pen, then he bayed
toward heaven again. I heard
neither words nor notes, only
a shapeless cry. He could not
bring forth the tune he heard!
Dazed, all I could say was,
"Delius, what key is it in?"
"A minor, Fenby, don't be slow."

Fingers inky, spectacles blurred
by tears, I confess being blind
as Delius himself when I groped
for the sanctuary of his porch.
Of course, in time we learned
to bring forth his music, imagining
ourselves on cliffs in the heather
looking out over the sea, knowing
chords in the high strings were
a clear sky. But I shall never
forget Delius, a shrunken relic,
mouth opened in anguish, gripped
by the awful beauty inside him.

RAVEL AT SWIM

"The inability to communicate speech, writing
or music when the peripheral nervous system
is largely undamaged is called an aphasia."
—"Maurice Ravel: Aspects of
Musical Perception," by John O'Shea

Something dark has stolen the sea from me.
Always a seal in water, I found its
melodies and swam open harmony
through them. Now I flail. Nothing I do fits

the rhythms around me. *Swiss Watchmaker*
they called me for the design of my work.
Mere lover of wind-up toys, a baker
of sweets, as though elegance were a quirk.

Now the hand that holds forks by their tines floats
like driftwood on the sea of music spread
before me. It will not write down the notes
I hear like a gull's bent tones in my head.

It will not play what I see on paper
and know I wrote two years ago to be
performed one-handed. (That was a caper!
I loved having such limits placed on me.)

It will not sign my name. It tries to light
a match with the tip of a cigarette.
What is left? It took me eight days to write
a fifty-six word letter I have yet

to end, consoling a friend whose mother
just died. I do not want to be seen now
by anyone who knew me at another
time. Pure artifice, they said, missing how

my need for form affirmed the passions of
my heart. They must not see me with the link
from brain to limb severed and all I love
lost. Sheer formlessness surrounds me. I think

but cannot share my thoughts. I remember
every flower's fragrance, the taste of lamb
roasted for hours over charcoal embers
at summer bazaars, lips on mine, but am

powerless to express myself. Let me
be alone. Let me have the grace of pure
music in my head, where I hear and see
perfectly. That silence I can endure.

MENDELSSOHN AT THIRTY-EIGHT

"On 1 November 1847, Mendelssohn's condition rapidly
deteriorated. He experienced the first of a series of
strokes."
—"The Mendelssohn Family" by John O'Shea

I look back on the promise of my youth
(*Felix* the fortunate) and am so tired.
A boy in auburn ringlets playing fugues
for old Goethe, a boy with liquid fire
in his hands! I glimpsed myself in glacier
wind and flood waters under the slender
Devil's Bridge. I loved the wild allegro,
the clack of trains, wind in a seaside cave.
Swiss sunlight, Monti Albani's sweet air,
Loch Lomond. I found music everywhere.
Now some mornings I am too weak to fold
back my bedsheets. There is nothing I crave
as much as silence. Not even pine trees,
the rich smell of old stones with moss upon
them, or the sight of snowy peaks would please
me. Quiet, like the moment before song
stretched out forever. Stillness, that instant
before strings quiver. This is what I want.

PAGANINI AND THE
POWERS OF DARKNESS

She swore an angels' chorus
swarmed her pallet bearing
sycamore slats for the belly
of her unborn son's violin.
When others claimed to hear
Satan's heartbeat in his sweet
tremolo, she remembered ebony
for Niccolo's fingerboard landing
like grace around her. It gleamed
with the Lord's truant light.

He said she was not to speak
of that, nor of his packer
father playing mandolin
to the rapt child curled
by the fire. She must lock
his early scores in a strongbox
under her bed. Let them believe
a demon composed the music
in blood. Let them weep
for the brilliance of his
fiendish cadenzas that flickered
like the tongue of flame.

An odor of sulphur rose
from the wings, sharp
as the whip of his bow.
Despite a hint of vapor
from below, no one stirred.
In a vault under the dark
stage he tuned his strings
to the devil's chosen pitch.
By shadow of candlelight, voice
hoarsened with cancer, he practiced
his sinister pizzicatos.

SAGE

"Why should a man die who has sage in his garden?"
—14th Century Proverb

He loves to see the purple whorls of sage
in bloom, its knee-high woolly branches white
at noon, their stalked green leaves seeming to age
toward gray in the relentless summer light.

From his bed with its garden view he thinks
of bees that feed on sage to make a prized
honey, of sage juice for joint pain. He drinks
sage tea to prevent night sweats and to ease

his trembling, uses a wash of sage to soothe
sore gums and blacken graying hair. Nothing
helps, but he feels there is nothing to lose.
Burnt sage for the room, sage on scabs, smoking

sage cigarettes for his lungs, sage with roast
duck to cut the fat. He does not want to
live forever. What he wants is almost
more than he can say. A year, maybe two.

COFFEE

Between me
and the Keystone ferry
crossing Admiralty
Inlet
is a pane of glass
etched
with the Nazi
cross,
drooping blood-red fuchsia
among brambles
where a hummingbird hovers,
one short stretch
of parched grass,
and a deer
staring without fear
as I slide back the glass.
Perhaps she cares
for hot oat bran as much
as I do,
or is as partial to
Schubert at such
an early hour that she
forgets stealth
and dares
come so near.
I raise
my steaming mug and smile,
glad to be still
alive for this autumn day
after three
long years
of being ill,
glad to sip her good health
while
she ambles
gracefully away.

FIRES

Your ax nicks
chips for tinder,
splits a block in two
strips that please you
with their kindling
power. Next you sink
the blade so deep into
a thicker log it stays
in place as you lift.
I listen to the pock
of wood on brick as you
work the last stakes
of oak free and sit
back on your tawny
haunches, breasts exposed
where your robe has fallen
open, waist-length hair
tucked into my faded Brooklyn
Dodgers cap to save it
from the flames that will
come of this.

In my hand, one long slip
of bark you peeled
for its scent rests
like a second skin.
I could not be
more ready for your
touch, but wait to watch
you light the day's
balled news of chaos
in Kazakhstan and poke
the blaze with a forked
madrone branch. Soon there
is fire between us
again and more heat

than we can bear.
Our shadowy pattern
flickers on the peeling
wall. My body fills
with warmth where it is
touched by the glowing
of your fires.

TOUCHES

The sesame oil
you brought for me
to knead into your skin
makes it glisten
in the firelight.

I want to be chaste
and slow with you
now, touching circles
from your pulse points,
calling the blood up
to your surface,
using my hands to bring
ease to your body

hidden here
and there by
a vermilion edge
of quilt.

The sound you make
is new to me and I
think of the sound high
tide makes at the moment
it yields to the ebb
current, a sighing of sea
water under the tug
of a quarter moon.

I do not break
touch,
pouring more oil
into the cup
of my palm, knuckles
still to your spine

and realize
it is you
who touches me,

who anoints the dry
places, touching somewhere
nothing
has touched before.

DIZZY

Dizzy Gillespie playing "Endlessly"
brings back those last slow hours together.
You're wearing a silken dress for me
to take off in the fading September
light, your long hair in my mouth when we kiss,
and the muted trumpet's chirps mark a time
that never seemed to pass. It's all mixed
together and slowed as in dreams. Now I'm
mixing batter so it can't be night.
You hold a glass of guava juice and it
catches the warm Indian summer light.
You hold out a palmful of freshly picked
berries and their darkness blues the pancakes
we eat to the blithe shamble of the horn.
The way the song skirts its own sadness makes
me think of the way we refuse to mourn
our parting. Again the way you hold me
while the mountain reddens with alpenglow
and Dizzy Gillespie plays "Endlessly"
tells me everything I want to know.

LIME AT THE EDGES

Lime at the edges,
a world washed in citrus light
as though spring
burst
this year on the brink of time.
Something to do with looking
straight
at the source.
Something to do with breaching
the thin sheath
of air, a season given
over to
more heat than ever before.

I do not like being still
this morning
here where the river
bends west but I must
rest
a while in the gathering
wind.
Where is the belted
kingfisher
hovering over water
like a hummingbird?
Where is the tiger
swallowtail sipping nectar
from the blackberry
vine, or the silver salmon?

I need to see the pale gloss
of false dawn,
hues
well-known from a life
by the sea.

I need something familiar
              seen
from the corner of my eye,
something the color of faith.

       Lime at the edges
with not even a hint of blue.
    I may have looked
    too long last night
        at the full
moon in all its glory.

CURRENTS

The great blue heron rides a cottonwood
limb downriver. She spins through a circle
of sunlight as her mate's wide loops dazzle
the morning and his hoarse squawk says he would
join her if he could. He swoops close to see
again there is no room. She turns her long
neck slower than the limb turns in the strong
current, keeping him in sight as though she
imagines currents of air mimic dark
river currents she will dare when the time
comes. He moves like a dancer past his prime,
a beat slow for her and just off the mark,
but game while she waits against the measure
for a moment they can enter together.

BEAUTIFUL LILY

Close enough to touch a sky given back
by the still surface, to catch the hopscotch
of dragonflies and one shadowy hawk
chasing a final shaft of sun, you watch
the young Comanche waterlilies fold
their yellow petals together. The night
tells them to hide their blooms in your pond's cold
heart till morning calls them to life with light.

Night-bloomer splotched sudden pink like the Pearl
of the Pool, you tell me your secret name
in return for mine, quickening the girl
christened Beautiful Lily as she came
alive by light of the moon. Nothing to
hide or fear. I too come open to you.

POPPIES

For years after a blaze, tree poppies
will spread brilliant yellow flowers
like the echo of flames in chaparral.
Camouflaged among crumbling bones of earth,
the pale salmon petals of pygmy poppies
thrive in thin alpine air. I have seen
acres of Oregon rainbows given over
to blind buds in hot southern sunlight,
cream cups tip their teeming bowls under
a sundown wind and prickly poppies turn
back cattle grazing a north Texas pasture.
I have been where winter rains stitch
a patchwork of Amapola del Campo
on the spring countryside. So I love
the moment your eyes close, when you become
the fire poppy whose buds must droop
before its flushed flowers will open.

CAPE LOOKOUT

You know the path the way I know the sea
so I am eager to follow you down
through morning mist. You move before me
like the spirit of light, the sheer energy
of your laughter capturing the sea's sound.

You know the path the way I know the sea
calling us here until we had to be
lying together where the breakers pound.
Through morning mist you move before me
and I know nothing makes you feel as free
as being held in the grasp of the land.

You know the path the way I know the sea,
the way our bones and deepest dreams know we
must visit each other's most sacred ground.

Through morning mist you move before me
toward a switchback, long legs striding surely
over the earth beneath its old-growth crown.

You know the path the way I know the sea.
Out of morning mist you turn back to me.

DANCING IN THE COSMOS

At first I thought the new
moon was pulling us straight
toward the cosmos in bloom
and singing at your yard's
edge. Then I heard the tune
rising. We began to swirl
in a warm whirlwind, sheer
scarves encircling us
like the visible scent
of snapdragons and sword
lilies all crimson, pink
and yellow where your hillside
buckles valleyward.

A sudden shift in tempo
let us spare the lacy
crowns of fennel bent
to our waists by the weight
of their seeds and left us
meshed in raspberry vines.
One look and again I knew
we would soon be hopelessly
deep in the feathers
and petals of the cosmos.

But I believed the music
filling the night was saying Give
in, spin through the cosmos
with faith we will not harm
even the palest wildflower
with our inspired capers.
I believed because the clear
sky we slept under this summer
was still teeming with wild
harmonies. Bats swooped
to owl shrieks and the Milky

Way soaked up the moon's
last offering of light.
So the land was going dry.
So the sun was hotter than ever.
Such nights, such alien dancing,
and never did we lose
a single frilled floret.

FLOYD SKLOOT's first novel, *Pilgrim's Harbor,* was published by Story Line Press in 1992 and his first full-length collection of poems, *Music Appreciation,* is forthcoming from the University Press of Florida in fall 1994. His poems have appeared in *Harper's, Poetry, Shenandoah, Priairie Schooner, The Gettysburg Review, New England Review, Virginia Quarterly Review, The New Criterion, Northwest Review, Poetry Northwest* and elsewhere. He has been a poetry fellow of the Oregon Arts Commission and the Oregon Institute of Literary Arts, and writer-in-residence at Centrum, in Port Townsend, Washington, and Villa Montalvo, in Saratoga, California. *Poppies* is his third collection published by Silverfish Review Press.